Not Yet Transfigured

Not Yet Transfigured

Eric Pankey

ORISON
BOOKS

ISBN: 978-1-949039-26-9

Orison Books
PO Box 8385
Asheville, NC 28814
www.orisonbooks.com

Distributed to the trade by Itasca Books
1-800-901-3480 / orders@itascabooks.com

Cover art: "Dais" copyright 2015 by Suzanne Moxhay. Used by
permission of the artist. www.suzannemoxhay.com

Manufactured in the U.S.A.

ORISON
BOOKS

CONTENTS

I.

II.

III.

IV.

V.

for Jane and Robert Atkinson

I.

THE TRANSIT OF HERMES

In the sudden rush,
One cannot behold
The logic of the loom

In the cloth's deep folds
And swathes. Blurred
Motion, a trace

Like a disembodied voice
In an elaborate fugue,
The unverifiable duration

(Neither solution nor
Resolution) of a note
Diminishing, pulled

Through the vanishing
Point like a thread, which
Once through, vanishes.

INTERIOR WITH OBJECTS

The bowl at eye level
Conceals its contents,

If it contains anything
Beneath its lip's
Narrow ellipse.

Varied, unfleeting,
Light solidifies

Over and outside time,
An octave range from
Ochre to delft blue.

The gathered objects
Gather permanence:

Bowls, jars, tins,
And ewers arranged
As if the skyline

Of a classical city,
Ideal, without flaw,

Not yet populated.
The function of each building
Still to be imagined.

LANDSCAPE AS ELEGY

Beneath the iron truss bridge,
Shadows overlap and merge,
Ride the deep creek's moving surface.

Sioux quartzite spires rise
As palisades on either side
Somewhere in South Dakota

Forty-odd years ago.
My friend—I just learned he died
A few days back—

Is the first to jump.
Then two other friends
I haven't seen in twenty years.

They each take another turn
Before I get up the courage
To plummet feet-first, submerge

And touch the rocky bottom.
Memory foreshortens
And what's near looms.

How easily I can block the sun
With the palm of my hand
Yet the landscape doesn't darken.

A HORSE FOR GUSTAF SOBIN

Filled in with a clay and ochre mix, the horse
Leans a little to one side as if to turn, or suddenly stumble.
A reed-blown black of manganese and charcoal suggests
The sweep of its mane,
                                its mud-spattered hindquarters.
All it would take is a bone burin or antler point
To engrave a single line, but no horizon distinguishes
Sky from land or scales the distance the distant horse crosses.

REALIA

In the diorama's replica world,
Artificial light mimics storm glow
On the stage of a prairie.

Wet sheets slouch on a clothesline.
A tornado touches down
On the curved horizon,

Still miles away.
Debris and wind have not yet
Reached the here and now.

Through the unglazed window
Of the makeshift shelter,
A lit lamp sits on the sill.

Behind it, realia in viscous shadow,
An ambiguous space where, we are asked
To imagine, a life is lived.

A THREAD OF SUNLIGHT ON EURYDICE'S HEM

Call it *an exercise in restraint:*

The angle of ascent is sharp
Like the sloped ceiling
Of a closet under the stairs.

The space cramped,
                    confined,
Ill-suited for the work at hand.

What should one expect
To emerge from an emergency:
A tabooed body?
                    A revenant?

What should one expect
Having forgotten the effects
Of isolation on memory,

Having forgotten the guile of ghosts?

Even a child,
                    running ahead,
Turns back to assure he's followed.

THE TAKING OF CHRIST

Amid the disquieting rush,
The various permutations
Of a moment are isolated,

Carved out by lamplight.
Contorted figures
Emerge like bas-relief

From an irrational, depthless
Space. The soldiers' armor
Reflects like rain-wet char,

Like the moonlit ribbon
Of a slug's trail, like mother
Of pearl. Jesus, embraced,

Leans back, fingers folded
Not in prayer, but interlaced
So as not to be torn asunder.

Homeless, displaced, the exile
Holds his ground. Nevertheless
He is easily taken away.

A MEMORY OF POPPIES

Like the darkest note a lute sustains,
Or the image of fog,
An index of emptiness
Condensed on film,

Like a single thread picked from a skein
(Not the thread so much as the care, the dexterity
Of leaving the whole untangled),
Like obdurate moonlight,

Like a refrain's insistence,
Like windblown snow in a cranny,
Or how, the moment before a movie starts,
The small audience

Takes in a breath all at once,
Like fascicles bound with a darning needle.

THE CHRONIC TRAVELLER

He prepares for the usual
Time travel conundrums:
The not-quite-taut surface

Tension that is the present,
How shallow events seem
Without accrued meaning,

Without memory of them.
He follows the coastal highway.
All his car mirrors are adjusted

But cannot account
For the blind spot
Where the past and future hover.

He watches rain fall,
Listens to the wipers' metronome,
The tide as it tugs back at the moon.

He drives to the scenic overlook
Before a sign exists
Saying *Scenic Overlook.*

STILL AND ALL

Over the narrow road's rain-filled ruts,
Clouds pass—the way sodden, tawny with muddy runoff.
The road rises as it bends, curves down onto
A waterlogged bog backstitched with limestone—
A place not blighted,
                                    but bypassed.
Then one's eyes stray to the passage
Of sunlight ahead, to, in the rearview,
A yellowish, purple bruise of sky. The storm,
A glancing blow, is soon enough forgotten.

SCRUTINY

How does one align the spectrum of wavelengths
That equal a white rose petal impaled on a thorn
(A white without the yellow of alabaster or limestone,
Without the blue of dry snow) in this shallow depth of field
Only a lens could contrive?
                                    And in the time it takes
To ask the question, one must confront the bleed-through
Of theory, the title written in graphite on the verso,
The obsolete method that rendered the image,
The paper decaying in its own acid. To preserve
The image, it is stored in the dark and rarely on view.

DISUSE

It was the end of something—
A fertility cult, for instance,
Associated with the bull.

Here and there, a hoard of bone pins,
A cache of socketed tools,
Hazel arrow shafts, chert points.

Each object fulfilling, it seems,
A ritual and thus magical end.
Preceded by a lull in gold working,

The bottom drops out of
The trade in linen and cloves.
Fish traps, made of twisted

Wefts of alder and birch,
Collapse and are preserved in silt.
A system of writing, finally perfected,

Falls into disuse during the plague years.
A passage tomb is unearthed.
The hardwood forests are felled.

The silver pigment refined to render
Rivers and streams radiant on maps
Quickly tarnishes to an acidic black.

II.

ÉTUDES

for Charles Wright

> *... I forgot about our emptiness*
> *And believed a shadow a thing of substance*
> —Dante

We do not speak of the dead and they return the favor.

Easy to miss the dust behind the decimal point.

The waterfall, frozen, is still, and yet the sound of falling water.

In the dream the interpreter was not *signing* but *sighing.*

With a breath, coals enliven, brighten and glow.

Half-set the moon flattens: a dollop of solder on the ocean's edge.

A bit of mercury splits and splits again and again splits: each drop
    a perfect planet: all ocean and light and storm.

From an alphabet, the universe is spelled out.

Skeletal and luminous, birches interrupt a green dark.

We did not enter the wilderness—it surrounded us, surrounds us.

A broken window mended with paper stains the room with a foxed, anemic light.

Don't forget the extreme pleasures of possibility within a set of rules.

The perfume of a sleeping child's hair, the slack ease of her body as we lay her down.

The objects of the still life remain; the arrangements change.

Upended, noon tips westward: nothing is explained.

Silence accumulates and illuminates the bottles, tins, and canisters.

To remain inconspicuous, we resort to elaborate camouflage.

Words are lost but the grammar endures like a hard vein of
    basalt. To placate a ghost, leave the cabinets open.

The road gives way to gravel then dirt then uneven parallel ruts.

Smoke that calms the swarm darkens the honey.

A din and flash of angel wings reflects in the just-thawed creek.

During the ceasefire, the hospital is bombed.

The mind is a just-thawed creek disturbed by a din and flash of
    wings.

With us, amid the ineffable, is the *nearby*, the ordinary we tally
    and classify.

Rilke's list goes like this: *house, bridge, fountain, gate, jug, apple
    tree, window.*

A view unobstructed: that which is at hand and homemade.

Like a tri-fold screen, silence divides a room. A ferment of wasps
among figs.

Place a grid upon the celestial curve; make of the vernacular an
arcadia.

A bone bobbin, a bone needle: still wound, still threaded.

Unscathed by crow caws, rain plays a five-tone scale.

Shadows are tacked down with thread.

As the peak slopes into fog, ripples reabsorb into distance.

What we said we said as an aside; no one else on stage heard a
word.

Not reaching escape velocity, of course, makes other matters moot.

The hummingbird, not weightless, expends much energy
    seeming so.

A water moccasin, mistaken for a vine, slips from a branch,
    almost within reach.

Red slivers halo an annular eclipse, cast crescent shadows upon a
    wall.

Soon waxwings will amass in the holly; until then the hard
    berries ripen.

The first spiritual exercise is to translate longing into
    disappointment; the second is to translate disappointment
    back into longing.

The nest, stitched entirely out of vowels, is shredded by hail.

We know God indirectly the way grass knows the scythe
    indirectly.

Stars cast out their banished light; a raised hand can block the
    sun.

One smiles upon lighting a candle, whereas blowing out a candle is a solemn affair.

Who, in a garden, does not listen to an articulate serpent asking apt questions?

At the confluence a red-winged blackbird balances on a reed.

Shadows dawdle for the briefest duration and move on.

We listen to the clatter of the loom on which the heavens are woven.

A rough braided cord of honeysuckle bark grows long enough to coil.

Degrees of grays recede: *barn-wood, overcast, tarnished-silver, offshore-mist, salt-glaze, slate, graphite, iron, charcoal, pewter, dove, drizzle* . . .

An archipelago of islands, a dash of scattered ink.

How bright suddenly the day: lightning with a stag in its gaze.
We bring our own bad luck with us like a set of jumper
cables.

The dancers as they dance follow a chalked diagram; the dancers
as they dance scuff away the diagram.

A screen allows us to see without being observed.

We divine with a *Y* of witch hazel: water rises to touch the tip.

Reindeer moss beneath coastal jack pines scums a granite ledge.

In the sutra's parable, a sparrow is offered a crumb, then sparrows
arrive from every which way: this is the chaos out of which
order is shaped.

A ceramic fragment calls forth its absent parts, conjures the slip,
the glazes, the fired clay, the empty space once contained.

Zero had to be invented before we could start back at zero.

In place of a face: a stylized gold foil flame.

The air is minutely transformed by the passage of an arrow.

How quickly magic drains from an object removed from its ritual
context.

Begin again with what is deemed unknowable.

With a shed antler, write in cursive script upon water.

To pray is to pry, to get a word in edgewise.

III.

GLYPHS

The middle of nowhere.
 A single contrail dissipates.
The measured silence is song.

   : :

The saint holds up
 His own flayed skin
As if a cloak, as if a gift.

   : :

Four of the six folding screens
 Painted a transparent gray wash
Stand in as the emptiness between peaks.

   : :

Like a explicit story,
 The footpath up to the headland
Begins and ends.

   : :

The horizon, after all,
 Is not a line,
But the arc of a continuous circle.

: :

A gorse fire.
    The ground ungrazed,
But not gone wild.

: :

The tide delivers up
    A drowned boy's body
And is willing to reclaim it.

: :

Shifting, impermanent,
    Uncluttered by soot:
A blue blur of incense.

: :

The task is over
    Before it is begun.
Perfection: a book without words.

: :

Here and there,
    Memory adheres: low clouds
Displace the habitations.

: :

How does one emulate
    The divine with only
A body to embody the disembodied?

: :

After thunder in the canyon:
    A measured silence
Pinpoints the middle of nowhere.

WINTER MEDITATION

Cold moves from the extremities to the core,
And there it burns sweetly at first like whiskey.
Enjoy the tidal warmth while you can.

The body is a good conductor of cold
And yet somehow an ice age came and went
And just now you feel your heart slow a little

Packed as it is in ice.
                    You dig into the snow
For shelter and, if not for shelter, to preserve
What you can of this moment as it might have been.

ONE DARK NIGHT

Beneath iron filings of stars,
The folds of the falls—moonlit,
Gravity-pulled—
                unfurl and slip.

From a great height, water spills.

A skirr of birds in the understory.
A barred owl plummets and strikes.

Caught off-guard, the owl's prey
Mistakes—
             or is it reconciles?—
The quick clasp as sudden insight,

The flash of pain as transfiguration.

DESCENT INTO LIMBO

Gray is permeable,

Absorbs shadow and shade
With equal ease:

                  the cinder gray
Of anvil dust, the shivery gray
Of graphite, gray
The density of clay,

Rain and greasy soot
To make a gray ink,

Infinite gradations,
A leaden spectrum,
Untinged by, purged of,
Color:

           the gray quarry pond

Out of which
A bloated body is lifted.

THE DEAD CHRIST

Although an angel supports it,
The dead weight has twisted, slipped,
And slumped.
              The candid torture—
Curated, marked upon the body—
Is held up on display.
                       Notice moonlight's
Glib effects: feet blackened,
Face gray and gaunt, each gouge
Blood-crusted, lusterless.

The chalked moon is like a god,
Which is to say: secret, silent.

THE DEPTHS OF AUGUST

I was blinded by grace,
A prey torn from its shadow,
Entwined only to unravel.

Alive in a dead calm,
I was fire from which
Air is withheld,

A charged element.
An illegible signature,
I was that which

Serves to conceal.
An inaccessible room.
Lightning dividing a sky.

CROSS REFERENCE

The perfume's aroma lingers
In the empty bottle.

The river pulls at its banks,
Conveys rich soil elsewhere.

Two notes allow a duration
Of silence between them
To be heard.

The tree of life has its roots above,
Its branches below.

Two smoke rings
Merge and dissipate.

Ellipses stand in for the *left unsaid*.

DUSK SEEN FROM ABOVE

A grid underpins even the field's neglected corner,
While fog—pervasive, incalculable—

Suggests the impermanence of phenomena.

::

I have abandoned the pursuit of the sublime

And am thus estranged from privation *and* vastness,
Subsumed again by depiction and description.

::

A map rearranges the landscape so that
Neither the map nor landscape is legible:

Simultaneity unfolds as succession.

::

Having grown insensitive to the barely

Perceptible vibrations of circumstantial evidence,
I fail to notice night backfill the dusk.

A STONE ATOP ANOTHER

One fills in the shadow, careful to preserve light—the place—or
    the memory of it.

As if clamor could scar. As if ink, irreversible, bled. The scale is
    enlarged so nothing

Remains, or can remain, hidden: a bird nest in an abandoned
    glove, for instance, or an hour-long exposure

Of the nearest star through a camera's pinhole. The deer, fear in
    flight, is not a ghost or guide, but embodied hunger.

To approach God, one places a stone atop another as an altar:
    the first step of a never-finished staircase.

IV.

LINES

The curve of a vase repeats the line of a shoulder.

Thought is not reliable, but if not thought, what?

Crisp light. Cold air. The willow wands in wind flex and tense.

The silver threads a burin uncoils are swept up into a nest.

Memento, we say, meaning *to bear in mind*.

A fortune is squandered on a feverish trade in tulips.

Pine, bamboo, and plum: ice inches into the river.

Nothing will be as before. With a wet rag the chalkboard is
    wiped clean.

ASTRAY

There is another word for this.
I arrived here *via*. I found myself astray.
The birds, omens of randomness,

Scuffled over the millet thrown down.
I followed a path of *et cetera,* carried
My own death like a stifled yawn.

The mulberry upheld the sparrow
As the cicadas' racket shriveled.
Heat awaited a remedy of wind.

Who scattered the millet about?
Who left an irregular trail of *et cetera*?
The mulberry stood empty, tenantless.

Amid the random, I found myself astray.
I stifled a yawn as if I might choke on it.
I arrived *by way of.* There's another word for this.

HIGH DESERT GLYPHS

As sun edges past noon,
A shadow scrim is coaxed
From beneath a boulder.

: :

Sky. Mountain. Cloud.
A path made by walking
Gullied by sudden rain.

: :

A cut bank collapses
Above a dry streambed.
Aspen-shiver. Dragonflies.

: :

What do I know?
The names of some things.
A song or two.

: :

Virga frays to the east
As birds skitter in scrub.
Talus holds its slope.

: :

Narrow river canyon.
At the brink, a worn rope
Cinched to a post.

: :

Contrails. A valley below.
A trail crosses
The creek seven times.

: :

Whose beauty is past
Change? Hills darken.
The clouds move on.

THE WISDOM OF SERPENTS

Shaped by gravity, a flame is not weightless.

The two signals, both weak, interfere with one another.

A brush fills with ink it cannot hold.

No one would mistake a maple leaf for an oak, a tulip poplar for a paw paw.

Rubbed away with turpentine, the delft blue is purplish.

There is a word for this pain wrought by distance.

Such an ungainly fruit, the paw paw.

One awaits an auspicious omen: a ring of mushrooms, say, or an open-ended rebus.

The changing light sharpens—no—blurs.

THE PROCESSION TO CALVARY

I have what one would call a bird's eye view.
A raven's perhaps. Three occupy the upper third of the sky,
High in flight amid the clouds. Another roosts

Atop a breaking wheel. There, twenty feet up,
Rags that once clothed a man snagged on cracked spokes.
Five more ravens circle in the distance.

Below: a densely populated valley, an oblong basin
Where crowds are gathering for the spectacle
Of a public execution in a landscape littered

With gibbets, hanging gallows, and a couple of crosses.
By the time Death arrives, time itself is an anachronism.
But I get ahead of myself. A dug hole, into which

A third cross will be wedged, awaits the condemned man
Who hauls (but has fallen beneath) the rough-hewn contraption.
Small acts of kindness continue. A peasant hands up

An equestrian soldier's fallen hat. The two thieves
Are not made to walk, but are trundled in a cart
To their execution. The soldiers, of course, given their javelins

And boredom, rough up the crowd more than is needed.
A scuffle has broken out among some spectators
Who have waited half the day beneath gathering heat

And a threatening sky for the carnival to start.
In the foreground, far from the killing mound,
Some mourners mourn the foregone. A mother? A lover?

A sister perhaps? They only have to turn around
To see what I see, poised as they are on a rocky ledge above the
    hubbub.
A black and white dog, hackles up, looks back as it runs away.

A PACK OF HOUNDS

The tracking shot through the winter forest
Matches the pace of a panicked deer
As it lunges through low branches.
The whitetail, circled and seized
Upon by the pack, stares at the viewer.

The day grows into itself as a milky
Northern light gives way to icy fragility.
Cloud shadows recast the solidity of the range.
One grows easily numb to the violence,
But not the intimacy intimated therein.

A TWO-DAY CIRCUMAMBULATION

53°5'0"N, 9°35'0"W

Bees in the fuchsia.
Hollow limestone underfoot.
    A hint of turf smoke.

A spider's web,
Anchored at opposing points,
    Billows and collapses like a sail

Where wind finds its way
Through a chink
    In a tumbled wall.

A ragtag grid of stone-bound fields
All the way down
    To land's end

(Or is it the water's edge?),
To the tides' push and pull,
    The marriage of sea and sky,

Of lapis and gold.
A raven feather
    Lifts in wind, resettles.

THAT WHICH IS IN-BETWEEN

The overloaded boat, turned back, sank.

As one remembers, the notion
Of memory itself is questioned.

Without attention being drawn
To the trap door's unequivocal presence,
The play ends.

The word *gift* is translated as *that which is in-between.*

Compared to the future one imagined in the past,
The future that arrives disappoints.

A point pierces. Tugged, a barb is set.

SANDIA MOUNTAIN WILDERNESS

A dawn of pines. A day moon
As dull as a scratched monocle.
Water seeps through rock.

The range, a depthless surface,
Is pink with feldspar.
Midway down the rift

Fallen rocks bridge a gap.
The mountaintop, once
A sea floor, is embedded

With fossils: horn corals,
Crinoids, and gastropods.
Unseen until it moves,

Dappled against the dapple:
A whiptail lizard.

STUDY FOR A GHOST

The space is still. Not empty.
The space is still not empty.
The word for it close at hand
Yet out of reach. The space
Is still. Empty. No. Not yet.

: :

Time slows down like an eddy in a backwash. The wintry light
fails to illumine each object, leaving some suspended, some
waylaid, some spectral. My brother, long dead, occupies my
dreams. Borrows money. Needs a lift. I owe him, he assures me.
The unrounded, almost two-dimensional flames of the driftwood
fire flare, hover, unattached. On the test, the blank was not meant
to be filled in, thus the instruction, "Leave the blank blank."

: :

The ghost neither trips the wire,
Nor activates the motion sensor.
As a result, the camera captures no image.

: :

The room is henceforth of no consequence. The hour held within,
neither receding nor advancing, is inert, and in this, is typical of
such hours in such rooms. The room is empty. Or rather, the room
is emptied except for an outdated calendar. The door is ajar. Or the
door is about to open, but facing the window I do not see the door.

The walls of the room are rain. It is as though I am underwater and each sound arrives amplified and distorted. I can aspire in the room to knowledge of nothing and be rewarded. One day remains un-X-ed on the calendar. The room, not spacious, holds the cold of palaces.

: :

The river runs fast with thaw.
The sky, heavy with constellations,
Slumps like a ceiling's wet plaster.
Time is, as always, beyond rescue.

: :

A ghost is a guest offered little hospitality. The consistency of melted wax, a ghost is more a liquid than a gas, more an unsteady focal point than the distant sound of a lute being tuned, or dry snow spun up by wind into a fugue. A ghost is an object around which time does not congeal. Yet *to haunt* is *to frequent*, even if infrequently. The brief span of a waltz in an abandoned dance hall is not enough to call forth a ghost. A ghost does not betray a trace of itself in a mirror's shallow depth. A ghost, like a cloud, is not weightless, but no brass counterweights in the felt-lined case can balance the scales on which it is measured.

TO FORMULATE A DEFINITION

To make of the self a void,
You smear yourself with ash,
But instead of disappearing,

You leave footprints behind
On the kitchen's slate floor.
The coastline cliffs collapse;

Loose threads of rain
Unravel from a cloud sampler,
But what is the proximate cause?

You learn to discern patterns
And predict the vernal equinox.
You hold a curve of willow charcoal

And make a hesitant first mark,
Then write a treatise
On the nature of things.

V.

LANDSCAPE IN THEORY: A MEDITATION

i.

One has been given a detached view: the mismatched edges of faded pinks and greens arranged in, or rather, as a coherent composition. Yet to call it a *vista* suggests one would care to look: a scruffy edgeland, interrupted by the curve of an off-ramp; a factory downwind from a reservoir; industrial parks and warehouses; the quarry filling with inky water. Occupied space gives way to empty ground. The road peters out, it appears, into a schism of woods. Of course, the land is bound by one's apprehension: the field of view aligned with a visual field. One feels, nonetheless, as if one has been blinkered, numbed by the artifice of perspective, the fiddly details, the convention of a consistent vantage point. The place, although mapped, is stranded: remote, unverifiable, an appendix tacked on like some final reading of a parable, or, like an agenda as yet to be determined, an afterthought after all.

::

The border, however tenuous—a brink of sunlight between two showers—must be imagined by each who crosses. What is to be found there? The crossed hands of the betrothed? A horned spirit extorting tolls at the crossroads? No. A sawhorse someone sawed in half. In the chain link, memorial crosses braided from roadside witch grass.

::

How does one distill from the ineffable an intoxicating yet subtle perfume? There are traces of fault left, test patterns and barcodes, a boreal birch forest buried by lava. Memory is like a fog nothing can scuff or sever. From a screen of static interference, the light fails and the dark reemerges. History begins again between two rivers. The context is withheld or held within: the categories muddied, the slippages slipperier. Was it snow hung in the plum's branches? Or the sticky silk tents of caterpillars? New accounting systems are put in place. A distinct knot is tied to tally each tide.

: :

One must exit at the last exit, trust a bridge suspended on echoes. The smallest species of white-tailed deer live in the pineland of the Keys. Beyond the mangrove's prop roots: a coral and sea grass wilderness. Listen—an instrument to mimic the sound of rain. Or perhaps it is the rain.

: :

Above rough coral bones, clouds open. Objects are farther than they seem. The light bends and what is beyond the horizon is somehow visible, a mirage: the light elusive, ever-changing, and yet one expects of it fidelity.

: :

The new development, the figment of it, is stilled, as if one had suddenly exited or were about to arrive. The schematic rendered in dull blue pencil overlays a composite: aerial views taken from different altitudes. The actual site has not been determined. The look of *nowhere in particular*, or *here*, but *here sometime in the near future* is the look aspired to. Ridges appear as depressions.

A basin inverts to a mound above the grade. The landfill, filled, will be planted with native trees. Roads will divide and connect the monochrome lots. Shadows will root objects to the ground. The distance will be kept just as one keeps one's distance from it.

: :

Wilderness, that mercy of something vast, takes over the arable land. To discern the thicket's order, subtract, now, the dimension of time. Leaves and vines, in place of language, emerge from a mouth. Endless loops and exhalations, split seconds and measured hours reanimate desire.

: :

The mid-summer sun all evening at eye-level. A white enamel bucket by a partly opened door. Wind in the cow parsley. A stack of old floorboards pried up. A jar of nails. The moment is weather-driven, yet no rain falls to fill a bog cut. How easily a photograph hoards all one merely glimpsed. At the holy well: a fleeting glance of far away, the water's bell tone on limestone.

: :

Stray bits of thought. No legend. No grid of longitude and latitude to attenuate this unattended landscape.

: :

Above the Shannon, the starlings' evening murmurations, a pure medium like mercury, all transcience and transmutation, continue to torque and agitate as a twisted cylinder, as acute curves. There is no surface to see beneath, only a malleable density and depth, a flailed flail, an unwound winding sheet. Involved and involuted. Volatile.

ii.

Surf thuds deep in a wave-hacked cave. White half-moon fossils imprint gray limestone. Gulls taunt and chuckle. Sightings are taken for accurate alignment. The sun, as it does, stalls at noon. Interstitial fauna of marine sands shift. Wind recalls its antecedent. The world arrives as rhymed. Blackberries, bilberries, rowan, and sloes.

: :

Rising sea levels nudge the glacial till bluff landward. High up: mare's tails, parallel contrails diminishing against a scratched sky as opaque as cobalt sea glass. Sea level rise nudges the four-hundred-million-year-old stones landward toward the salt marsh and lagoon they shelter. With each wave the cobbled beach clatters. The shifted stones lift and shuffle.

: :

Blue shadow on a Provencal hillside. A worker with two walkie-talkies in his hands shouts across the distance to his co-workers. Emerald glints on a pigeon's breast. Another worker, walkie-talkie in hand, shouts back. As in Ruskin's "Sepia Sketch of Leafage," light ambers the vine's full green.

: :

In the given world, between the ellipses, one notes the corollary of pond ripples and planetary orbits, the compression and release that is *motion*, the time-lapsed dispersion of a storm front as the menacing clouds enfold into a tracery of mists. One lives at the edge of the world, although it feels like the center.

: :

The auroras are an unstable spectacle, collapsing even as they rise like a sinking ship buoyant on air that water quickly displaces, an elaborate wreckage lost as the surface heals over. Flames shiver between opacity and transparence, static-abraded, effaced, then translucent, solid, seen-through as one sees through the Milky Way, a congealed mass of light, a hive of hollows held together by geometry. The insubstantial pageant—a baroque turbulence of randomly initiated ratios, a diaphanous lightness like water ripples preserved over time in stone—cools from rose to green, apart and parting, gaps in torn curtains, asymmetrical intervals hung as virga, as falls, as sheerness without edge or chasm, and is reabsorbed back into the black cold, into the icy scald and sear, a congealed glaze that snuffs and smothers any light that might try to escape it.

: :

Depth is conjured by way of elaborate angles on a miniature's flat two-dimensional space. No shadows cast. No highlights. Bent beside a stream, the god tastes the stylized water: the blue of his hands and face the blue of the cool clear river. Walls far and close in focus. All that is continues. Does not recede. Does not move. The epic length of a day beheld in a single glance.

: :

Obscured as one might say of light-fall. Or a distance haze hides. Each note is held, but at a whisper, as when dancers take the stage and the curtain opens and it is not yet the first day of creation.

: :

The *white* of the magnolia. A repertoire of rusted objects. The celestial bodies' calibrated but unseen influence upon one's fate. The ocean lighter than the sky. The eighteen flame-like points of the staghorn sumac. Sunrise through acidic humidity. Space compressed through a concave lens. An arrow-pierced saint tied to a tree. A sketch of a fletched shaft, of the tree alone without the saint.

: :

The way home—overlapping trajectories—resembles some archaic cursive used only for the holiest of texts.

: :

A few days remain nailed up on the calendar. Where the plot diverges, one misconstrues a turn toward closure. The vast map of the frontier is refolded. One ignores the gaps and is moved neither toward improvisation nor reiteration. All one ever has is a partial view, a view *on-the-cusp-of*, a view *not-yet-transfigured*. Like drizzle beheld from afar, a cloud appears to descend.

iii.

The dark closes in. The moon emerges, enlarges the *out-there* into a ghostly space without dimension. The book of the night sky is redacted, charred like a burnt field, reduced to carbon. In the window—adrift, detached, disorienting—an oasis of reflection.

: :

Inside, a mirror hangs at an odd angle to its reflection, undermines the plumb and the level. The window overlooks a gibbous moon in a leafless willow. Each object is dusted with the residue of cast shadows, with the *once-was*, the arcane. Keats says he is *content to look on the mists of idleness.* Autumn is the longest season, albeit blurred and crepuscular. *In the midst of idleness* is how one misremembers it.

: :

The autumn sky, after all, fills in the space between branches, expands as the mass and volume of leaves decrease. One turns the hourglass over, but cannot restart time. A little dune accumulates beneath the cinch.

: :

The dull overcastness of the day registers as *mute.* The wood's edge obscures the view, if it is not itself the view. How quickly evening gathers like weather beyond the line of oaks. The picture plane's narrow limitations give way to an illusion of depth, an *into* that just might be entered, and entered—the air flecked with moss spores and leaf dust—surrendered to, a shade absorbed into shade.

: :

Stark, low winter light. The creek rough with thaw. The day moon is to the eye what an echo is to the ear. A scaffold holds up a single cloud.

: :

One is offered a glimpse, a narrow slice of landscape framed in the instant before the train doors close. The roads and paths lost beneath snow. Around one, the murmur continues like conversation exercises culled and dutifully repeated from an out-of-print textbook. And when the train next stops and the doors open, the view is *another*, meaning at once *different* and *the same*. Thus the unresolved tension, a feedback loop of damaged recovered data, is recurrent more than constant, its intended function exhausted. As if to recall a long-forgotten presence—some uncertain state between emerging and disappearing—one has set one's sights on what extends beyond the pictorial field. On the tip of one's tongue (meaning *what lingers just out of reach*) snippets of a folk song sung to see how, once circulated, it returns changed.

: :

One looks out to the slick slabs of coastal mud flats through a window's fragile filigree of ice and finds the low tide an alloy of pearl and mercury drawn taut in the offing. Or one looks up at stars and back in time and finds a chart to fix a point in space. One tests the limits of sight, senses all that is beyond the senses, has faith in an argument augmented by aught.

: :

In a clearing, one longs for the forest's depths, subdued blue hues of amnesia, but finds instead a past, a landscape salvaged from memory's wreckage. A ruined stone foundation tilts inward. The river continues to freeze and thaw. Surface ice shatters and cants, freezes once again to offer a jagged passage across.

: :

The borderline, a coast, constantly shifts. The destination is shadowed, hidden by the location marker.

: :

Beneath the inky wash of winter dusk: a snow-covered hedge maze. To see even this much one must extend the exposure so that highlights amass on the surface of a dark shallow bas-relief. A path is all that remains of the passage.

iv.

One awaits the triumph of Pan as one story is grafted onto another. The delight of repetition modulates easily into the horror of repetition. The sky glows as neither dusk nor dawn. The bouquets in the foreground have been traced from a naturalist's miscellany. The central tree is charred, scarred by fires that never quite caught. Buried like a grub, the past mutates.

: :

One draws on memory but the flimsy surface tears. One enters the fold through the stile of a *therefore*. Therefore, a river is an errant arrow to the oxbow. As rational as a cloud, one settles for a tentative equilibrium. The river quivers in the wind, in the unquiet light. Quarry scalpings, field stones, erratics . . .

: :

Presence annuls absence and, like memory, is incomplete. How rare for the eye to rest *here* and not on the view beyond: the wash of soot where nothing quickens or disturbs the wet, dark membrane of loam that is this turned field.

: :

Sediment accrues and shifts. A tree fledged with jarring grackles empties. The afterimage fades on one's retina: an adagio afloat on a moment of pause. How otherworldly the rescued refugees swaddled in their silver foil emergency blankets.

: :

Without key or grammar, one understands the balance and impermanence of the dry stone wall. The break in its length, experienced as a *gate*, opens onto fields and beyond: slow sinuous lines of other distant stone walls, roof angles, sun-bright panes, an overgrown cherry orchard. One places a hand on the stone and expects to feel a reservoir of night's cold and mineral damp, but already the stone has absorbed the morning sun's heat.

: :

A forty-degree angle is formed by rain and the roof's incline. One does not hear the web tear, but looks up at that instant and sees the web torn. Steam lifts from the iron. A window fogs. In the garden, a child traces with her finger the curves of reflected distortion upon a gazing ball.

: :

More often than not, one must break a trail into the depth of trees, part the dark as one might dig up a black slab from a bog. One stumbles in the midst of the scathed forest, regrets having entered the dense thicket lit only by a filament of light that is one's own body aglow.

: :

Streams. Runs. Kills. A ramble of runoff. Beyond or behind—a geometry of *neither nor* or *either or.*

: :

The stream pools then accelerates as it slopes toward the falls, beyond which a hazy horizon merges a tree line with sky. Power lines drape across the expanse. Time is embedded in the layers the moving water excavates. Two birdsongs overlap. Harmony like happiness is transient.

: :

The irrefutable changes day to day. With only tides to tell time, the standardization of minute increments is a nearly impossible task. Once measured, the hours in between become distance, the distance a scaled map. The tide stalls before it turns. The length of that stall is a single unit. Day to day the irrefutable changes.

v.

Today, the rain-light shifts incrementally on the birch bark's papery flecks. A door opens to high water in low-lying areas. To order is to inquire; yet one is left at last with what is discernable. Out in the offing, there's a lull in the rain, a sea surface full of clouds. The net's grid of loops hangs slack as it is pulled from the depths. As is often the case, the concealed is revealed, or vice versa.

: :

The whole day is lost suddenly to headlights. Rivers one crosses go unseen—the Salt, the Skunk—beneath the narrow sway and rattle of bridges. The air's mineral, acrid, above the hard, cracked fields. Tonight, the night is all rain, not yet falling, elemental, gathering itself until it breaks.

: :

The crystalline edge of smoke is a fossil of fire, a stain, a reminder of previous marks, an absence, say, commemorated by what replaces it. One element merges into another. One observes, and deliberately so, adrift in the ordinary. The light, an agent of clarity, scatters—partial, insubstantial. No need to deduce a narrative, to see the incomplete as a depth dredged up or gouged out, or to consider the pragmatic urgency of gravity as an impetus—the push and pull of ropey lava, cooled millennia before wind or water—that constant solvent—reveals again horizontal strata, an inbuilt balance. By the time the postlude concludes one has forgotten the prelude. The scar does not fade as promised. The bridge freezes before the road, which leads to an interior no baroque detour can diverge from. The grid of the window frame is set down upon the table as shadow. There cakes of wheat and honey, as bright as gold ingots, float just above the stoneware plate, its white glaze chipped and crazed. The outside enters the house as drafts. As leaks. As a door blown open. One comes under a room's spell. Memory as well embellishes.

: :

What is there to do but dowse beyond one's own understanding? The landscape is not travelled *in*, but *through*, as through a maze of sun-dapple: the vertical never quite plumb; the horizontal at a tilt, off-kilter. A cloud frays at its edges like a single leaf from a sutra. However much sifts through—unnoticed, unclassified, or unarchived—weather is the common denominator. How much energy must be spent tracing the river to its source—that trickle amid an array of rocks? Where one finds oneself is nowhere, really: an in-between space: a series of vacant lots—unmown, gone to seed—like a sentence cluttered with auxiliary verbs—not far from the motel where the jury is sequestered. One entered without an exit strategy. One entered with one's shadow as a casual companion. One is lost yet lucid. Lost and lucid. A spectator, one sets the parameters of the scope, of the scape.

: :

The solace of amnesia must be that one lives in the present, concerns oneself with weather, and not weather patterns. There must have been years of plenty when the clutter gathered in drawers, hope chests, corners, attics, and cellars. Wallpaper comes loose at the seams. Memory—inconclusive, elliptical—is a shrine of sorts, a quiet aftermath. The past, like fire, assumes mutable shapes. One makes do with available light. A needle is threaded; a table is cleared. Again delayed, one awaits the forthcoming Rapture. The thread frays. The needle rusts.

: :

Too late to the bacchanal, one watches twilight settle as lees, dregs, and sludge. The foundation is poured. The construction delayed. Rust inches up the bulldozer's blade. Wind rocks the boom crane's jib and hook. One keeps uncovering something one has known all along, and is taken aback by the reminder, by how easily something slips from one's mind, that one ever had a purchase upon it in the first place. The worksite, once a field of clover strung with spider web, a fringe, out of focus, yet pearlescent, darkens beneath humid cloud-shadow. One notices how the dim light heightens a sense of presence, as conversely the mundane is elevated by one's attention to it: a swallow twinned by its reflection in a wheel rut's puddle, the sag and curve of a slack rope, the crazy weather out of sync with its season.

: :

One had hoped to isolate the singularity of *the place at that moment*, although one never doubted the impossibility of the task. The moment is lost, the present present only for *this* present. A note is sounded and gone. The radio, tuned more often than not to static, offers a wordless ghost story, a mantic white noise. It's easy enough to miss the signs and portents of one's death. Words get in the way of such a substanceless transmission. Telepathy is what one is after, even if one must bang it out—the long and short of it—as a telegraph of jittery code.

: :

Sometimes a flame detaches from its fuel, leaps over a swale and the prescribed burn is anything but. That's what the sunset looks like just now, flaring up as it does, at this southernmost point.

::

A line marks each day, not to commemorate, but cross out. The moss-crumbled brick rejoins the clayey soil as flakes, slivers, and dust. To hide a blood stain the entire cloth is re-dyed maroon. Impermanence takes its form as repetition: sunrise, moonfall. The mountain sheds ice-melt. Streams and rivers swell. Here and now, space and time, figured as a single equation. One suffers from an amnesia that sets in after a war, but notes the legible beneath the blur of the wiped-away.

::

Inasmuch as sleep descends, tomorrow's iteration of fog will lift from the surface. If one dreams one dreams of water—of a river that winds in wide arcs across a dark floodplain; of rare Venetian honey from flowers periodically submerged in lagoon tides. Adrift, without the knowledge of the depth beneath, one perceives the stayed tension of a storm far off in the distance. But no clear border, endpoint, or landfall. A bit of blue borrowed from Piero della Francesca flashes, but little else reaches the surface. The dinghy is the width of a stretcher, the width of a grave—each a bed of sorts—afloat on the deep.

ACKNOWLEDGMENTS

Bear:
Descent Into Limbo
Landscape in Theory: A Meditation *[Inasmuch as sleep descends . . .]*

Belletrist:
Landscape in Theory: A Meditation *[One must exit at . . .]*

Bellevue Literary Review:
A Thread of Sunlight on Eurydice's Hem

The Bennington Review:
Landscape in Theory: A Meditation *[The solace of amnesia . . .]*

Cincinnati Review:
Glyphs
Realia
The Chronic Traveller

Copper Nickel:
The Transit of Hermes

december:
Cross Reference
Study for a Ghost

Diode:
A Memory of Poppies

Georgia Review:
The Procession to Calvary

Hotel Amerika:
Winter Meditation

Image:
The Taking of Christ
The Depth of August

The New Criterion:
Landscape in Theory: A Meditation *[The whole day is . . .]*

New England Review:
Landscape in Theory: A Meditation *[The new development, the . . .]*

New World Writing:
Landscape in Theory: A Meditation *[Above the Shannon, the . . .]*
Landscape as Elegy

Pleiades:
Landscape in Theory: A Meditation *[The autumn sky, after . . .]*

Slab:
To Formulate a Definition

Talking River:
Landscape in Theory: A Meditation *[Stray bits of thought . . .]*
Landscape in Theory: A Meditation *[The way home—overlapping
. . .]*
Landscape in Theory: A Meditation *[The borderline, a coast . . .]*
Landscape in Theory: A Meditation *[Streams. Runs. Kills. A . . .]*
Landscape in Theory: A Meditation *[A low horizon line . . .]*

Terrain:
Astray
Landscape in Theory: A Meditation *[The white of the . . .]*
Landscape in Theory: A Meditation *[The irrefutable changes day
. . .]*

Tupelo Quarterly:
Landscape in Theory: A Meditation *[In the given world . . .]*

UCity Review:
Lines
Landscape in Theory: A Meditation *[Inside a mirror hangs . . .]*
Landscape in Theory: A Meditation *[One is offered a . . .]*
Landscape in Theory: A Meditation *[The dull, overcastness of . . .]*

Valparaiso Poetry Review:
Landscape in Theory: A Meditation *[Too late to the . . .]*

A special thanks to the good people at The Dora Maar House and the Studios of Key West for time, shelter, and friendship. Thanks to H. L. Hix for his kind and considerable attention to a long poem here that has become not quite so long. Thanks to Luke Hankins and the folks at Orison Books for believing in this collection and giving it a home. I owe everything to Jennifer, Clare, and Karlyn.

ABOUT THE AUTHOR

Eric Pankey is the author of fourteen collections of poems and a book of essays. His work has been supported by fellowships from The John Simon Guggenheim Memorial Foundation, The National Endowment for the Arts, The Ingram Merrill Foundation, and The Brown Foundation. He is the Heritage Chair in writing at George Mason University.

ABOUT ORISON BOOKS

Orison Books is a 501(c)3 non-profit literary press focused on the life of the spirit from a broad and inclusive range of perspectives. We seek to publish books of exceptional poetry, fiction, and non-fiction from perspectives spanning the spectrum of spiritual and religious thought, ethnicity, gender identity, and sexual orientation.

As a non-profit literary press, Orison Books depends on the support of donors. To find out more about our mission and our books, or to make a donation, please visit www.orisonbooks.com.

Orison Books wishes to thank Eric Nelson for his financial support of this book.

For information about supporting upcoming Orison Books titles, please visit www.orisonbooks.com/donate, or write to Luke Hankins at editor@orisonbooks.com.